Paying Taxes

SARAH DE CAPUA

Children's Press®
An Imprint of Scholastic Inc.
New York Toronto London Auckland Sydney
Mexico City New Delhi Hong Kong
Danbury, Connecticut

Content Consultant
Margaret Heubeck
Youth Leadership Initiative Director of Instruction
University of Virginia Center for Politics
Charlottesville, Virginia

Library of Congress Cataloging-in-Publication Data

De Capua, Sarah.
Paying taxes/by Sarah De Capua.
p. cm.—(A true book)
Includes bibliographical references and index.
ISBN-13: 978-0-531-26040-1 (lib. bdg.)
ISBN-13: 978-0-531-26212-2 (pbk.)
1. Taxation—United States—Juvenile literature. 2. Taxation—Juvenile literature. I. Title.
HJ2381.D42 2013
336.200973—dc23 2012004790

Printed in the United States of America. 113

11 12 13 14 R 22 21 20 19

Scholastic Inc., 557 Broadway, New York, NY 10012.

Front cover: Couple looking through receipts

Back cover: U.S. money and tax forms

Find the Truth!

Everything you are about to read is true ***except*** for one of the sentences on this page.

Which one is **TRUE**?

T or F Postage stamps are a type of tax.

T or F Americans' tax money is used only in the United States.

Find the answers in this book.

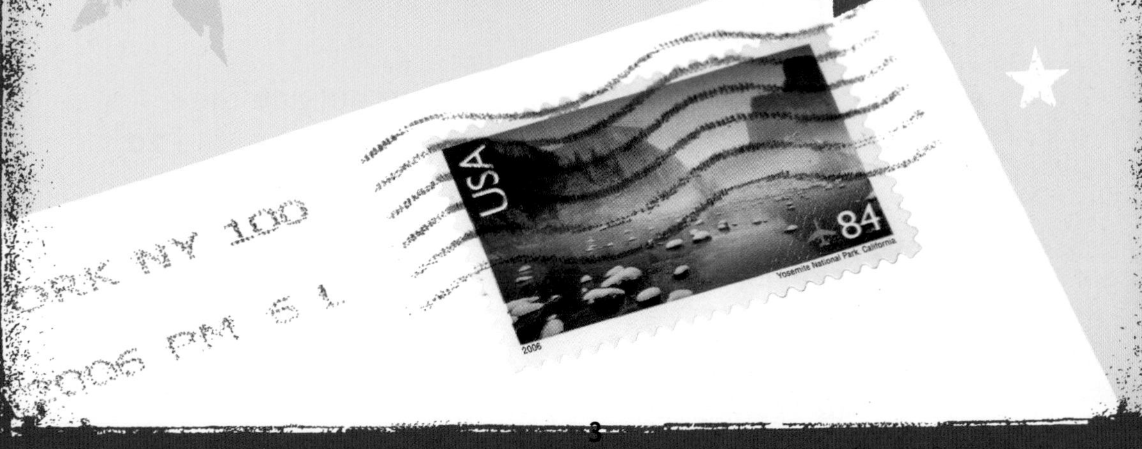

Contents

Property taxes in New York state are among the highest in the United States.

The U.S. Constitution is the oldest written constitution still in use.

15% JUICE

Paying the Government

Have you ever heard someone talk about paying taxes? Perhaps a parent or other adult mentioned taxes. People and businesses pay tax money to governments to help pay for a variety of important public services. The law requires people to pay taxes. If a person does not pay, then he or she is breaking the law.

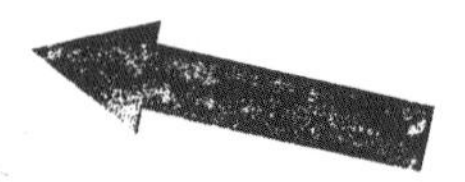

Many states charge a lower tax on groceries than on other purchases.

Providing Support

In the United States, local, state, and **federal** governments all collect taxes. Local governments are those of towns, cities, or counties. State government manages the affairs of the whole state. State government officials conduct their business in the state's capital city. The federal government is the government of the United States. Leaders of the federal government work in Washington, D.C., the nation's capital. Tax money supports all levels of government. Taxes provide the services that keep communities running smoothly.

The U.S. Senate and House of Representatives meet in the U.S. Capitol in Washington, D.C.

During the 1700s, men in Russia paid taxes on their beards!

Taxes are added to the price of every gallon of gasoline.

Taxes Everywhere

To collect enough money, there are many things that are taxed. Purchases such as video games, music, and books are taxed. So are gasoline and movie tickets. Some places charge taxes for food or clothing purchases. People pay taxes on the money they make at their jobs. This is called a personal income tax. People also pay taxes when they own large possessions such as houses or vehicles. These are called property taxes.

Homeowners pay taxes on the water they use.

Have you ever had to stop to pay a **toll** while you were riding in a car? You might have been crossing a bridge or traveling on a highway. A toll is one kind of tax. Homeowners pay taxes for the services they use. This means that phone, gas, electric, and water bills all have taxes added to them. Postage stamps are another kind of tax. The money from stamps helps support the work of the U.S. Postal Service.

Got Sense?

Sometimes, certain taxes may not make sense. In Texas, cowboy boots and hiking boots are not taxed. But rubber boots and climbing boots are. In Colorado, a cup of coffee from a drive-through is not taxed, but the cup's lid is. In New York, you can buy a whole bagel to go without paying tax. But if you plan to eat it in the shop or ask a worker to slice it, there is a tax.

TIMES SQUARE
CROSSROADS OF THE WORLD
ONE WAY
NEW
All Route South
SHARED ZONE AHEAD
W 46 ST
6678 M104
RIGHT LANE MUST TURN RIGHT
NYPD

Types of Taxes

As you can see, people pay many different kinds of taxes. The amount paid for each tax depends on a number of factors. Some tax amounts depend on the community or state in which a person lives. Amounts might also depend on how much an item or service costs, or how much money a person earns. Taxes on certain items can even be higher if an item is considered unnecessary, such as jewelry, or unhealthy, such as cigarettes.

New York taxi drivers pay a tax on each trip they make in the city.

Purchases and Property

A sales tax is paid when a person buys something, such as new shoes or an electronic device. The tax is a certain percentage of an item's original price that is added to what a consumer pays. For example, a shirt might be marked $10 in the store. If the sales tax is 5 percent, then 5 percent of $10, or $0.50, is added to the price. The customer ends up paying a total of $10.50 for the shirt.

Some states, such as Delaware, do not charge sales taxes.

Property value can be affected by the location of the property and any changes made by the owner.

Anyone who owns buildings or land must regularly pay a property tax. Some states require property taxes for boats, cars, and farm machines, too. Property taxes are based on the value of a piece of property. Property tax is usually a local tax, which means that the money funds the local government. Often, property taxes make up a large portion of a local government's funding.

Excise Tax

If you purchase a **luxury** item, such as jewelry or a fur coat, you might have to pay an excise tax. Excise taxes are sometimes also placed on harmful items to discourage people from buying them. Alcoholic beverages, certain unhealthy foods, and cigarettes are among the products that people must pay an excise tax to purchase. The government hopes that such taxes will cause people to think twice before buying things that aren't good for them.

Tariffs

Tariffs are taxes on products that are **imported** from other countries. Tariffs make American-made products more affordable by comparison. Tariffs are also paid on products that are **exported**. Tariffs imposed by other nations make American products more expensive in those countries. As a result, the products become less desirable there. Different countries impose different tariffs, depending on what products those countries export themselves.

Tariffs are paid on any items that are shipped from other countries to be sold in the United States.

Income Tax

All U.S. residents must pay federal income taxes. Most state governments also require residents to pay a separate state income tax. Residents pay a certain percentage of their overall incomes, or earnings, minus certain **deductions** that the government allows. In general, Americans who make more money from their employment must pay a higher percentage in income taxes. People who earn less pay a lower rate. Americans who fall below the **poverty line** or live off the interest from **investments** are often not required to pay income tax.

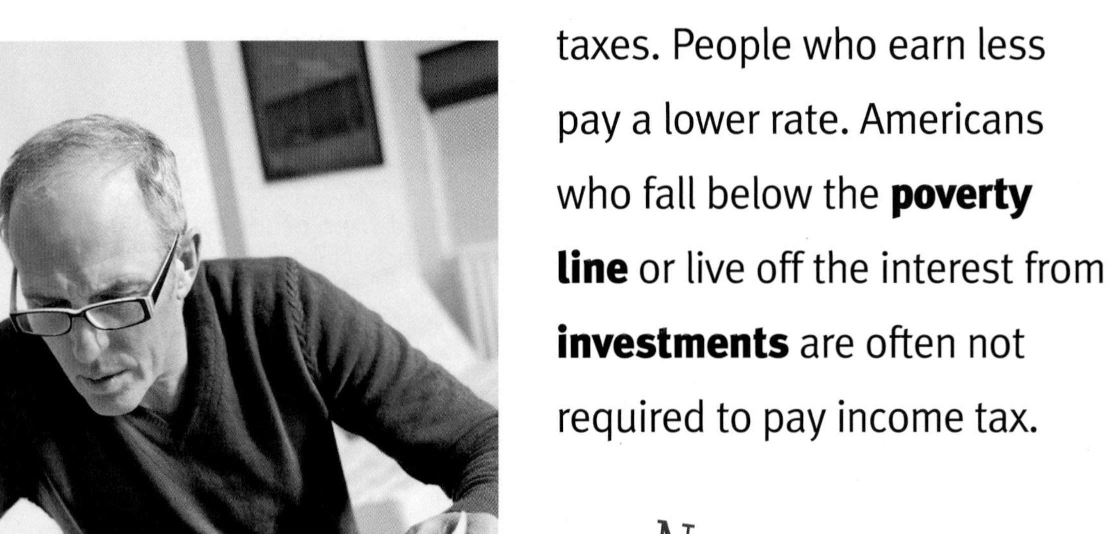

Nine states do not charge any income taxes.

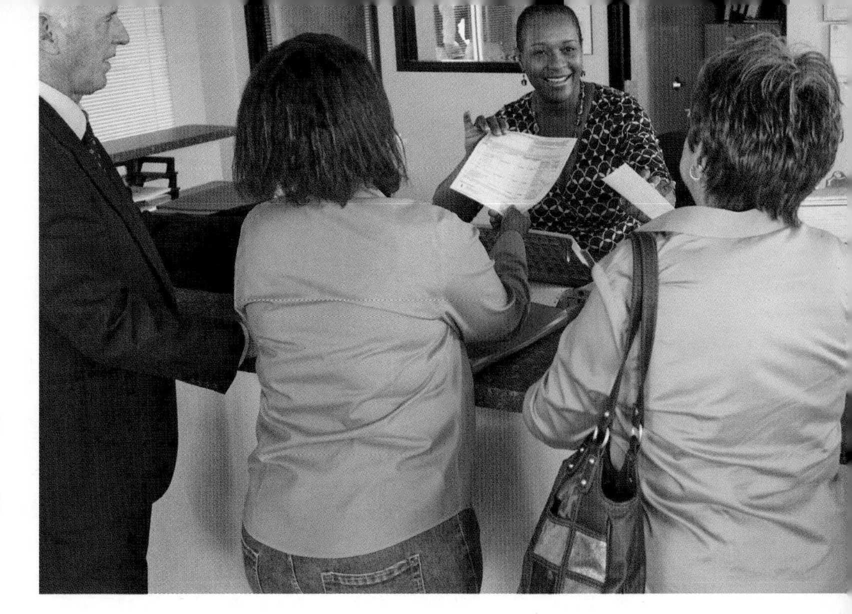

The United States has had an unemployment program since the Great Depression (1929–1939).

Other Kinds of Taxes

Workers also pay an unemployment tax and Social Security tax. Both are taxes imposed by the federal government to fund certain programs. People who lose their jobs can receive payments from the government for a period of time while they look for work. The money for these payments comes from unemployment taxes. Social Security taxes fund monthly government payments to people over age 62. Because many of these people are retired, Social Security payments can help them with their expenses.

Taxes Go Around the World

In addition to providing important services at home, the U.S. government also uses tax money to help or aid foreign nations. This help can be in the form of money, equipment, food, workers, or a combination of all of these. Less than 1 percent of all federal tax dollars are used for foreign aid projects.

The U.S. military maintains bases around the world, in such places as Korea, Germany, and Kuwait. These bases not only help defend and protect the United States, but also those countries in and near where the bases are located.

The earthquake and tsunami that occurred in Japan in 2011 required vast amounts of foreign aid. Relief came from the United States and other countries all over the world.

Haiti suffered widespread damage when an earthquake hit in 2010. Relief was rushed to the nation from all over the world, including the United States.

Aid was sent to Pakistan beginning in 2010. Nearly 20 million people were affected when the country was flooded following an especially heavy rainy season.

Firefighters are one type of public service provider that depends on taxes.

How Are Taxes Used?

If you take a look around your town or neighborhood, you might notice some of the many ways governments use tax money. Police departments and firefighters are funded with taxes. Public schools are also supported using tax money. Water systems, power plants, and waste removal services also receive government funding.

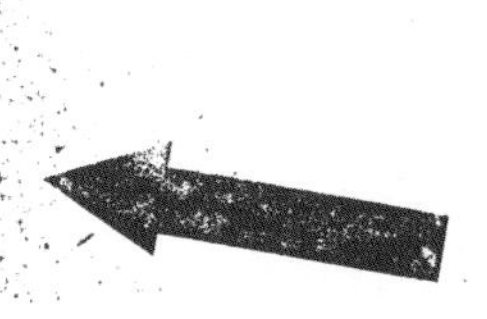

Seventy percent of firefighters in the United States are volunteers.

Local Taxes

Local governments use their tax dollars to manage the everyday life of the city, town, or county in which you live. Local governments use tax money to pay police officers, teachers, firefighters, and librarians. Taxes also fund the salaries of local government officers, such as mayors. Local taxes also help maintain public buildings, such as libraries, schools, and government offices. Property taxes are a local government's main source of income. Local governments also receive some funding from state governments.

Taxes help keep public libraries running and support reading programs for young readers.

State taxes help make attending a public college cheaper for state residents.

State Taxes

State taxes also help pay for important services. The construction and maintenance of state highways are funded by state taxes. The expenses of running the state government, state colleges, and state universities are also supported by taxes. This is why state residents do not have to pay as much to attend these schools. Some tax money also goes to help maintain state parks and natural resource areas. State police officers, governors, senators, and **representatives** are all paid using state tax money.

The U.S. Constitution gives the federal government the power to collect taxes.

A portion of federal taxes goes toward paying the president.

Federal Taxes

Elected officials in the U.S. Congress decide how to spend federal tax money. Federal taxes pay the salaries of important leaders such as the president, vice president, and members of Congress. It is also used to maintain U.S. government buildings in Washington, D.C., and pay the many employees who keep the government's operations running smoothly. Federal tax dollars also support federal agencies, such as the Department of Justice and the Department of Defense. The federal court system is also funded through federal tax dollars.

The U.S. military, space exploration programs, and national parks and monuments are all funded by federal tax money. Some federal tax money is also used to aid private businesses and industries. When states suffer the effects of natural disasters such as earthquakes, hurricanes, or floods, the federal government provides money and resources to help clean up and repair damage.

Federal taxes help protect land and wildlife in California's Yosemite National Park.

Tax Day

Each year, millions of people across the United States take part in tax season. Everyone who earned an income during the previous year must file a tax return. This form includes information on the amount earned and any taxes already claimed by the government, such as Social Security. It also provides information about whether the person is married or has children. Tax returns must be sent to the Internal Revenue Service (IRS) by Tax Day, usually April 15.

Tax Day is moved if April 15th falls on a weekend or national holiday.

A History of Income Taxes

The U.S. government did not always tax incomes. Congress first tried to enact an income tax in the 19th century. The first attempt, in 1862, ended when Congress voted to remove it in 1872. Twelve years later, Congress tried again. This time the Supreme Court declared the law unconstitutional, or not allowed under the U.S. Constitution, and thus it was removed within a year. It was not until 1913, when Congress passed the Sixteenth **amendment**, that the government was able to tax citizens' incomes.

Income tax was first enacted to help pay back Civil War (1861–1865) debts.

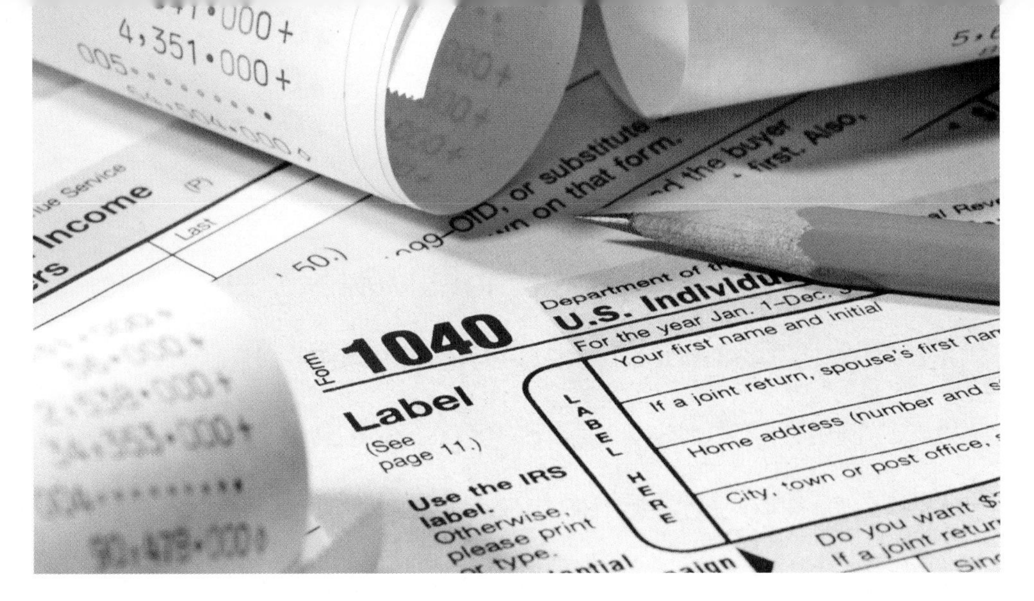

Much of the 1040 form can be filled out using information on a worker's W-2.

Filling Out the Form

These days, the tax return process usually begins when an employer sends all employees a W-2 form. This form includes the amount an employee earned during the year and how much was withheld for Social Security, unemployment, and other taxes. Taxpayers use this information to fill out sections of another form, called the 1040. Other sections on the 1040 ask for information on children, spouses, property, business costs, donations to charity, and other expenses.

Tax deductions for families help make raising a family a little easier financially.

Tax credits or deductions are given for many expenses. These credits reduce the amount a person is required to pay. For example, in 2011, a credit of $1,000 was offered for each child in a taxpayer's household to help cover the cost of raising the child. Tax credits often result in the taxpayer receiving a refund. Sometimes, a taxpayer owes additional taxes. This amount must be paid as soon as possible.

How to File

For decades, taxpayers filled out their 1040s on paper with a pencil. Then they mailed the forms to the IRS. Today, people can file electronically, or e-file. They might do this through the IRS Web site or with the help of computer software. Some taxpayers choose to go to accountants, tax lawyers, or organizations specializing in federal and state income taxes for help. These specialists make sure tax forms are filled out accurately and on time.

An accountant can answer questions and help find tax credits that might apply to a person's income taxes.

Breaking the Rules

The IRS reviews 1040s to make sure they are accurate. Sometimes a person makes a small mistake and the IRS corrects it. A taxpayer might not report all of the money he or she made during the year. If this was done accidentally, the person might pay a fine. Sometimes, the person does it on purpose to hide money made illegally or to avoid paying taxes. These crimes are punished with fines or time in jail.

People who hide large amounts of money from the IRS can be taken to court and sent to prison.

The Boston Tea Party

Sometimes people rebel against certain taxes. In 1773, the American colonies were ruled—and taxed—by Great Britain. Colonists particularly disliked the tea tax, which was added to all tea except the tea supplied by a certain British company. Many colonists considered this unfair and decided to protest. On the night of December 16, 1773, a group of colonists boarded three British ships in Massachusetts's Boston Harbor and dumped more than 300 crates of tea overboard. This "Boston Tea Party" and similar protests helped lead to the American Revolution (1775–1883).

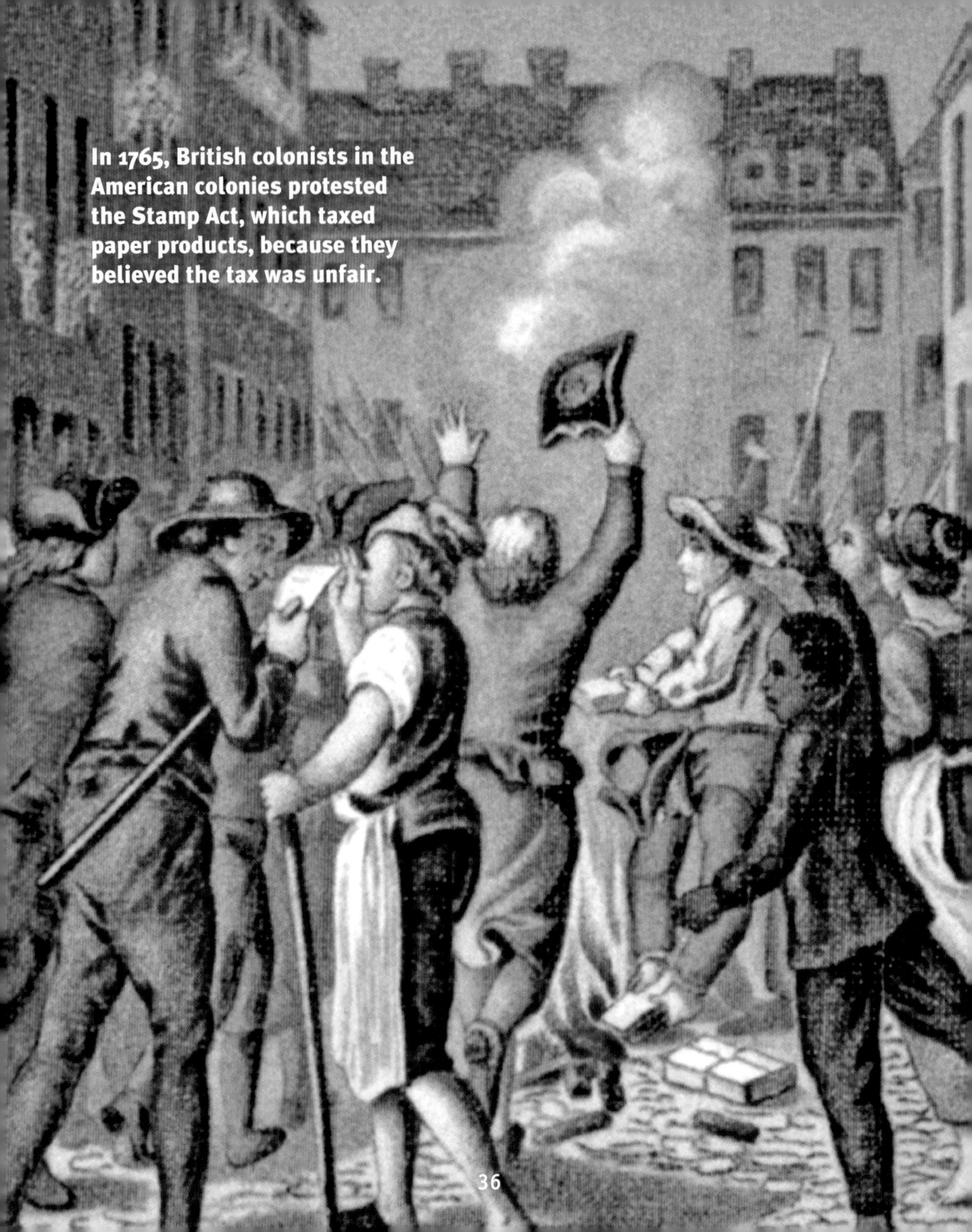

In 1765, British colonists in the American colonies protested the Stamp Act, which taxed paper products, because they believed the tax was unfair.

Judging Taxes

Taxes help people maintain a decent quality of life. But sometimes, individuals, organizations, or government leaders argue that a certain tax should not exist. Citizens and their representatives have the right and responsibility to protest taxes that they think are unnecessary. But how does a person know if a tax is necessary or unnecessary?

The Stamp Act was intended to help cover Britain's debts following the French and Indian War (1754–1763).

Questions to Consider

U.S. citizens elect local, state, and federal government leaders. These leaders help shape the laws that determine how and when people are taxed. These leaders also decide how tax dollars should be used. Citizens can affect tax laws by voting for **candidates** who share their views. When a new tax is proposed and voted on, citizens and government leaders must decide whether the tax is necessary or unnecessary. Citizens can also speak in support of or against specific taxes at town hall meetings, city council meetings, and in their general assemblies.

Americans vote for leaders who they believe will best represent their interests.

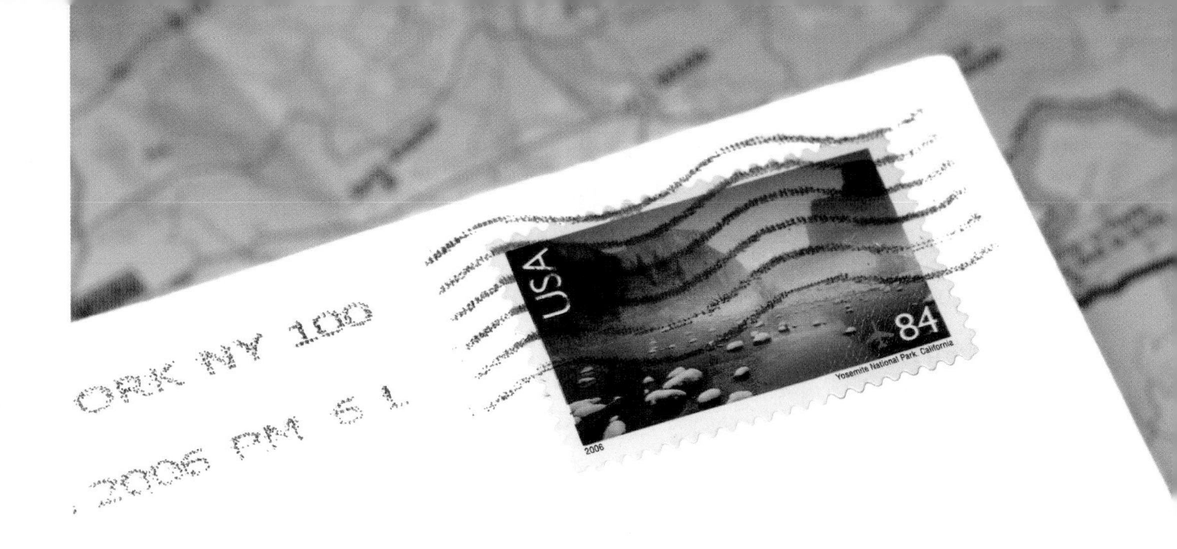

Postage stamps help keep the U.S. Postal Service running.

Serving the Common Good

One important issue to consider is whether the tax supports a service or program that is needed by the community. The postage stamp is one example. The money raised from these stamps helps pay the salaries of postal workers. It also goes toward the purchase and maintenance of mail trucks, sorting facilities, and post offices. Taxes that support police forces, schools, and roads are other examples that serve the common good.

Ability to Pay

For the tax to be effective, taxpayers must be able to afford it. This generally means that people who have more money pay more taxes. Income taxes are one example. Other examples are luxury and sales taxes. People who have more money generally purchase more products and services that are more expensive. As a result, they pay more sales and luxury taxes than people who purchase fewer or less expensive items.

A Tax Timeline

1700s

Men in Russia are required to pay taxes on their beards.

1787

The U.S. Constitution, which gives the federal government the power to collect taxes, is signed.

Ease of Payment

The tax should also be convenient for taxpayers to pay. This encourages people to pay the tax and makes it cheaper and easier for the government to collect it. For example, unemployment, Social Security, and certain other taxes are taken from a person's paycheck automatically. Sales tax is added automatically to purchases.

1895

The U.S. Supreme Court rules that a federal income tax is unconstitutional.

1913

The 16th amendment is passed, establishing federal income taxes as legal.

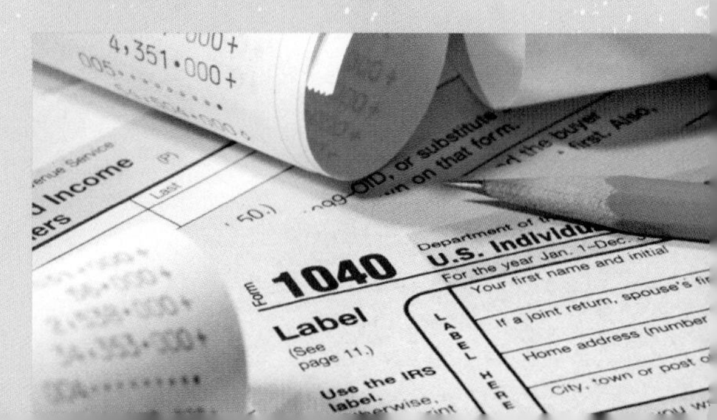

Helping the Economy

An economy is the way a country runs its industry, trade, and finance. Taxes such as the unemployment tax and Social Security tax can help support the economy by providing income for people who have lost or retired from their jobs. With that money, they can buy food and other things they need. This helps provide income to the people who supply those goods and services, which helps keep the economy going. At certain times, governments might raise or lower taxes in an effort to maintain a sound economy.

The Social Security tax supplies money to retired workers.

New England town hall meetings give citizens the opportunity to debate their taxation directly.

People Still Disagree

People continue to debate about which taxes are necessary. Sometimes individuals or organizations argue that a tax should be higher, lower, or paid in a different way to make it more affordable or more effective. People may not always agree with the taxes they pay. But obeying the law by paying taxes for necessary services that serve the common good is part of being a good citizen. ★

True Statistics

The section of the U.S. Constitution that gives Congress the power of taxation: Article I, Section 8

Amount of taxes collected in the United States in 2010: About $2.3 trillion

Amount of taxes refunded to individual taxpayers in the United States in 2010: About $358 billion

States with the highest personal income tax: California, Hawaii, Maine, Maryland, New Jersey, New York, Ohio, Oregon, and Vermont

States that have no personal income tax: Alaska, Florida, Nevada, New Hampshire, South Dakota, Tennessee, Texas, Washington, and Wyoming

State with the highest state sales tax: California

States that don't collect sales tax: Alaska, Delaware, Montana, New Hampshire, and Oregon

Number of words in the U.S. tax law: 3.7 million

Did you find the truth?

T Postage stamps are a type of tax.

F Americans' tax money is used only in the United States.

Resources

Books

Bedesky, Baron. *What Are Taxes?* New York: Crabtree Publishing, 2009.

Cheney, Lynne. *We the People: The Story of Our Constitution*. New York: Simon & Schuster Books for Young Readers, 2008.

Taylor-Butler, Christine. *The Constitution of the United States*. New York: Children's Press, 2008.

Visit this Scholastic Web site for more information on paying taxes:

★ www.factsfornow.scholastic.com

Enter the keyword **Taxes**

Important Words

amendment (uh-MEND-muhnt) — a change that is made to a law or a legal document

candidates (KAN-di-dates) — people who are running in an election

deductions (di-DUHK-shuhnz) — amounts that are taken away or subtracted

exported (EK-sport-id) — sent products to another country to sell them there

federal (FED-ur-uhl) — of or referring to the national government

imported (IM-port-id) — brought into a place or country from somewhere else

investments (in-VEST-mints) — things in which someone has invested money in the hope of getting more money back later

luxury (LUKH-shur-ee) — of or referring to something expensive that is nice to have but not really needed

poverty line (PAH-vur-tee LINE) — an established level of income below which a person is considered unable to afford basic essentials

representatives (rep-ri-ZEN-tuh-tivz) — people who are chosen to speak or act for others

toll (TOHL) — a charge or tax paid for using a highway, bridge, or tunnel

Index

Page numbers in **bold** indicate illustrations

About the Author

Sarah De Capua is the author of many nonfiction books for children. She enjoys helping young readers learn about our country through civics education. She believes every responsible citizen has a duty to make sure tax money is spent wisely by government leaders at all levels—local, state, and federal. De Capua works as a children's book author and editor, as well as a college composition instructor. She holds a master's degree in teaching from Sacred Heart University in Connecticut, and is currently working toward her doctorate in composition and TESOL at Indiana University of Pennsylvania. She has written other True Books in this set, including *Voting*, *Serving on a Jury*, and *Running for Public Office*.